Nobody's Ezekiel

Nobody's Ezekiel

and other poems

by Christopher Middleton

HOPEWELL
PRESS

Designed and typeset by Hopewell Press
Cover: Turtledoves, MS. 18th cent. Bibliotèque Nationale, Paris
Distributed by The University Press of New England

All inquiries and permission requests should be addressed to the publisher:

Hopewell Press
PO Box 633
Red Hook, NY 12571

Library of Congress Cataloging-in-Publication Data
Middleton, Christopher, 1926-
   [Poems. Selections]
   Nobody's Ezekiel and Other Poems / Christopher Middleton.
      pages ; cm
   ISBN 978-1-937679-54-5
   I. Title.
   PR6025.I25A6 2015
   821'.914--dc23
                         2015011261

Acknowledgments

Thanks to Carcanet Press for six poems from the "Interim" section of *Collected Later Poems*, to *PN Review* for another six poems, to *Poetry* for "The Flight." Heartfelt thanks to Zulfikar Ghose, David Wevill, and Marius Kociejowski for their good advice on wording in the drafts of certain poems. For two years of caregiving, love and thanks to Glenda McKinney.

CONTENTS

The Flight

Just seen, running, and silver grey
along the top tube of a fence between myrtles and me,
too slinky for a bird and even at this distance
unmistakably a quadruped and
nimble, some sort of unspoiled animal, but which?
It ran as if away
from a threat, peril was everywhere,
a footsole crunches it, it is mangled
by a tyre's treads, hawk scoops it, turkey buzzard
pecks at it, no speech mitigates its pains,
even the cat fools with it, until, inedible,
it is kicked into the gutter. There she goes,
the slinky silver grey Atalanta of reptiles
vanishes in no time, for the wind
whisks from her feet such tenuous gusts of air—
brisk now where turnpikes stretch their webs,
and not forever can an earthiness
so sweet as this propel such grace.

She'll have got to the mantis eggs by now,
at each gulp of hatchling
she slowly blinks with satisfaction.

The Typesetter's Visit to Cavafy

Admit me to your apartment, Sir,
dim as it is.
Tell me whatever you wish
or would invent (though probably not
for the boys with rosy lips) not only
for us future ghosts of those who flew
winged for their moment by a great soul.

I've knocked, when might you let me in? Now
captivity among the aged ages me,
painfully the past is now and real. You knew
how it revolved and for reasons of its own
played dead, omitting us, who dwindle,
easy to charm—and the beautiful are pitiless.

Your very phrasing, Sir, plucks from mud
epiphanies; not only gods
engender things that shine. Well considered,
your word for Fool and Stranger
reversed the plunge, flighted the dolphin.

I knock only once more. What should I do,
if you are out? I'll not wait until from some
smoky bar or nastier haunt you
hurry back home.
Up to your ironies I am not. How mild
you might be, there, horn-rimmed eyes
swiveling every which way;
but when your moment spoke, you were
the lamp itself.

How you did wangle your way
over chasms, step by step
where no trails led but those
you rediscovered, Sir, to kindle
anew shocks of recognition that had knit
their texts for ancient tragedies.
Resignation, now wink at it,
your charity lets go with a sigh,
and for Zenobia you had a heart.

The Spoils of Lowestoft

Blown from the steppe an age ago,
   all fuzz, doing its cartwheel,
the tumbleweed bowls across
   desert highways: flooring it
along the turnpike to somewhere else,
   you do not hear it click and crunch.

That is why I'm glad to remember
   the foghorns, their conversation;
the bulky luggers, their orange sails;
   through salt air the tread of boots
on the pebble beach traveling up
   to my pillow in the dormitory.

And now the lifeboat, unforgotten,
   solid craft, propelled or not
head-on it took those perils of the sea
   we sang about on Sunday, picturing
in their sou'westers the lifeboat men
   hugging the oars that they pulled back.

For today, time is the sea and not
   the river; into it you dropped
shallowest things, not to be recollected;
   then the sea one day throws them back
as markers; you bite your lip, the sea toils
   to fashion it into a moment's marker. Still

The spell of nervous tissue irks a soul:
        anxiously involved in the galaxy
it looked, they did say, for markers of a haven;
        and still it waves goodbye to a body
only to storm with the storms,
        harden in stones, rejoice in the animals.

Our Rain Crow

Car noi chanta auzels ni piula...
-Arnaut Daniel

How apt of this rain crow
as rain came pattering down
for our flowers on the fresh grave
to hoot from his haunted orchard
sotto voce twice.

Then a wave had crested, giving rise
to fields of force; foaming vortices
carpenter the island of Phaeacia;
liquid eye-beams, Greek and chisel
carve to measure the finest of ships.

'Some few accustomed forms,
the absolute unimportant':
thus E.P. on a distinct slant
(still at an early age)
plotting some real connections.

So it is, here for the oldest folks
who still can hobble by,
there is a dangerous dog proclaiming
his Ah Ah Ah. One rough day's ride
and the sea crashes ashore.

I see my orchard gone for good.
Antiquated, for a moment
reasonably trees revive. One single twig
or two blossoming would cradle
a twitter of linnets. Soon
the punctual cuckoo too must croak. If

a cherry reddens,
it is for air, also the choir
far out in France at first light
let fly with one voice overtopping all;
yes, in the accustomed form,
it was the oriole, his folded fluting
for dear life I now recall.

What sense do I make, shedding this skin?
Memory, had you none tougher hidden?
Ancient shipyard fantasm,
fantasm orchard, sacred ground;
the texture puzzles, there is disbelief.
I do perceive it, past denying
pedestals to my words, to our crow its rain.

The Hispanic Gardeners

It is always on Wednesdays
the same: extending long poles
tipped with engines, on two of them under
hats broad-brimmed to avert
the lash of a dogday sun,
they scratch a living.

From what they distract me
I never yet discerned. Simply
            from a deepening silence
I am drawn by a cap, colour of cream,
a neck-cloth fluttering
to the gardener's forward motion.
                Heavens above,
how I did admire foreign legionaires
who wore, just so, their képis,
and as I turned the pages fought to the death
such ill-mannered Africans.

I am distracted by this buzz
and click when a twig or tougher
grass-blade is hit, till now this mowing
had not called the scythe to mind,
and the busy skeleton.
                But for these gardeners
did a pool of bull's blood ever give off
from saffron sand a whiff of cinnamon?

Still, there's a gallantry gavottes
through their not knowing
or sparing it a thought, a gallantry giving
emblems the finger. And the grumble of labour
is heard in a far land
as the knock of a spoon on a dish.

My Father's Table

Two florins on my father's table
(it was a table, not a desk)
drew me not to the money
but to the coins themselves.
They stole into my thoughts
of Florence, of Leonardo.

Much, much later
the memory of these florins
draws my thought back
to the coinage of the Romans.
It was in those days I began
collecting bronze *sestertii*,
and little silver, just so long
as the denarius was imperial.

My father at his table
writing letters, longhand notes
for his book on music—
his pocket never full of florins,
sometimes he'd fish
big pennies out of it,
enough for the book I wanted,
Lord Tennyson's poems in it.

It was not much later that
an ever rarer florin
came shining from his pocket;
I'd bike to Mr. Whitacker
and find a dark *dupondius*.

You draw back to the past
we must fabricate with thought,
and the past responds, for real:
it eats our images up
as often as it is hungry. The more
I know the more I must forget,
and the past will push you on,
as the future pushes you back.

Another

Sun then coming down
dazzled
and on the wooden bench
the old man scans his boots

Someone walks by
to the right of him
only a silhouette
and it has filled his mind

bodily with her flowers
her garden and small hands
then sorrow comes afresh
her now being long gone

—anyway earth overpopulated
this consumption of identity
this old man
a thing of the past

A Hiding Place

And a man shall be as an hiding place from
the wind… as rivers of water in a dry place…
Isaiah 32, 2

They only thought there was
a hiding place
and then that there had been a hiding place
and then they discovered
the hiding place must have been hidden.

All this they thought, stupefied
by sentiments of revenge. Rancor,
it oiled their star-machine.

And all because they came to boast
that where all hell breaks loose
had to be the place, in their devotions
the hacking off of heads
cleared the way to paradise.

Well might we wonder
what hidden places they were coming from,
like anyone else. There is no calculating
the degree at which
perversion grabs the growing will to power.

Oh yes, great moves hide in time
and bide their turn. If healed, if green,
we do not listen for
perpetual rumblings, or see, in pleasant land,
the homes catch fire. Then,
then in their death cult
they had found their hiding place.

The Path Long Overgrown

What is this reckless
little thing
a magnet for

swept back wings
a tiny Concord

and a cat's whisker
sprouts

out of each nostril
of the pointed nose

Where the wings widen
a lightning bolt
bridges them

not a sound
one scorching zig

zag
long a portent
in these Navajo lands

and of what ganglion
turning and turning

a paroxysm,
the gaze unstilled
this fascination

knit with magnesium
blue tempers of acid

vaporous cage fixed
for the stiffening
animal and petty

intelligence starved
by the abstract—

Look now, she will sing,
how the mobs get going
daily quicker footstep,

of old, cottages to thatch,
the candle flame the porridge

divine things
always
further on.

From the Reveries of a Gentleman

Where can that good soul have been,
rain pelting, sun blazing,
with ink horn at the ready
by a tavern table, or else,
easy among cooks, barons, varlets,
he slept under the staircase in a château,
and sung to the lute, coming to be,
the music, weightless and strict,
he found in a snowflake.

How did Pergolesi fight his disease
just long enough, a spider's web hangs
in one corner of that room.

The ragtime composer spent nights underground.
I hope the customers had gone.
Air, now clearing of its gunshot aroma
from the whiskey, isolated
magically the fingers as they qualified
sonorities. Odd birds inhabited
the earthly keyboard, he only touched it,
to hear if the right notes had come.

All this I find myself wondering,
and something lumbers to the front:
I shiver, here it comes, I grit my teeth,
invoke an image for it--the stooped
crew carrying a marble frieze in the *Purgatorio*,
their crushing guilt, their griefs.

Again it brushes on past.
The spider can't tell night from day,
but will spin again.

To Exult with the Fireflies

Overhead, they were there
(and I was believing you);
above our dance
in the labyrinth, coitus.
Here they wove theirs,
the fireflies;
They had floated indoors,
they drifted, invisible,
into our cabin,
and could find
no way out.

They brought us nothing
of their universe,
but body with body, these
complete with airs and graces,
were brightening,
they, too, moment by moment,
abolishing shadow, you call for more,
the sparks go out, then turn me over,
to exult with the fireflies.

North Slope of Mount Ventoux

Red wines in their long time
have been misting the interior...

The rim is chipped, now there's a crack
running halfway down to the stem,
she said, and see here, in the curve
where the blower softly blew
and your wine glass bellied out,
there's the crack...

Not on your life, this thick glass
holds good. Look, how should I give up
my time piece, my travel book?

Real beauty resists time's passage,
new things don't set memories aglow again
for the fantasies to fool with.
Red wine in this glass from thereabouts brings me
the mountain, olive trees, the vines
modulating colour with the season.

I call up cherry trees long ago cut down,
I hear the voices of friends at the marble table.
I smell the fresh and smoked meats in the charcuterie.
When I open a door, here's the mulberry tree.

In this glass I tenderly hold
acres farmed, small cabins with red tiles
and the long straight ridge
our mountain gathers up its flank
and the weather horn that towers from its head.

Seeing Geese Arrive

For Miranda, my daughter in Colorado;
Vivid detail in a phone-call from her suggested the poem.

A full moon floated
on air in the twilight,

wrinkled lake below
splashing all of a sudden.

collision, confusion
when a formation of geese

from far off up north
flew in and landed

with such an abnormal
flapping and honking

you started to think
the geese had straddled

two currents, one warmer,
and the cool one beside it,

yes, a river ran though,
prompting alarm from nerve tissue

safe in the weathered goose breast
and sensitive as a testicle.

*

Ages ago they'd say worldwide:
Thus doth spirit crash into matter.

Davy Jones's Locker

With his boat full of harum-scarum chimeras,
Don't let him ever come back to our shallows.

So his nets are too heavy to haul in? Well then,
Take him a knife or chopper, cut the cable.

If you can get at it, and get at it you must,
Slash every net wide open, promise new ones;

Somehow or other, free the chimeras to wallow
All the way back to Davy Jones's Locker.

Down there, even a chimera can't speak. In '39,
I too heard U-boat engines throb
                              underway for the Atlantic.

The Crêpe Myrtle Calls for Piety

Summer breeze, gusting rarely,
snow blossoms to the tune of thousands
swing this way, that way—

delight of barbers,
white-haired old men and women
nod on benches, nod at nothing—

no clippers, no lotions,
rarely seen the host of bees,
how scrupulously, sucks and combs them—

Chant now, chant with reason, stings
do not startle you, without anguish
you come to the border. Myrtle tree,

bee and these your kin, Fortuna,
come their time, then bring them peace,
help them believe their work is done.

On the Gift of a Sea-Shell
from Vassiliki Papageorgiou

1.

They seldom say that God
Inclined his ear
To the cries of old men
From shaky patio chairs
When the Syrian military began
To shell their Aleppo souk.

And God's ear, they do say, could discern
Helen's footstep when
Sad at heart she came into sight
And on their bench of stone
As if copying spiny grasshoppers,
Sensing the heat again
The old men stopped their chirping.

2.

weil
Ohne Halt verstandlos Gott ist.
-Hölderlin

That in his young mouth he could taste
Barefoot among the ferns on his patrol
Blackberries picked from the clusters
　　Behind thorn stockades, tasted
　　On them the savour of salt for soon
　　There was the sea, the reef to explore,
And that his tent, nights, caught whispers
From the stream it was pitched beside,
He has given me warmly thanks.

3.

Brooding under the spell of language
Reckoning on bias in our attributions,
We know it was not Homer but Chapman
Who found that grasshoppers were spiny.
Wing-case and shank for a moment in mid-air,
Then touch flitted, ear was prickled,
And the right word was there.

4.

There was no rosy sanctuary for the shell
But a cavern of antiquity and its messages.
Into a hole in the wall the shell fits
And at the back of it a winding trail begins
To traverse century after century.
Once in a while I listen there
For Helen's voice. Papyrus, parchment,
Rag-paper, none has a trace of it. Hear now
The public voices howl nasally onscreen;
Sounds like hers fell through cracks in history.
Was her accent ever judged incompatible
With her radiance? When she spoke, some people
Only tried to catch a glimpse of her tongue.

Out of the sea-shell, no perpetual murmur;
Is beauty, as a rule, like deity free but latent?
Of a rare harmony circling Kekova Achim told me:
Poignant dialogue with a finch, let it go,
A condor will call, today will have come
Bringing to the island someone who can still
Speak as she spoke, sing, imaginably, like Helen.

Theory of Dust

Twin haystacks, one at a distance,
both round, shimmer
faintly gilds their tops, vestige
of summer light, summer helped
to store-feed for wintering cows,
shadow, shadow at the visible base
balances the stacks, blue pools of it,
blue from moisture.
                The cottage elsewhere,
forest rushes up to it, then
down, down the rock cliff the sea
climbs or crashes;
the light-house keeper lived there,
his Norman wife, his tin coffee pot,
and from their spouts, morning come,
a milky fragrance drifted, fainter
the older they got.

                Atlantic howl or smile, haystacks
were not torn to pieces, the cottage
was not crushed, each was a station
for the beyond that spoke all atmospheres,
for a logic mobile as fishes,
for a mystery doing its work.

Of the Event Among Willows

We'd thought she might pass away
like this, with a jest, but no—
having resolutely pushed
her walker up the gentle slope,
she set herself down on the seat. She had forgotten,
so had we, to apply the breaks,
back down the slope she careered,
until, as if slung from a catapult,
into the river she overturns.
Slip of a thing that she was,
the volumes of her summer skirt
made of her a nenuphar,
afloat, amazed, amused as by a gift.

These Volunteers

1.

The young, depressed, debonair,
what kinds of parents raise them
for groveling to the power of darkness?

Into a waste of hope,
into the ruins they'll go—
possibly Aucassin, possibly Nicolette.

Most cheated and lied to get there,
they found their track and took it.
This one and that, how will they quit?

2.

Impossible once, but these could survive.
Look, they line up, not one of them
less than upright, and there's one
the image of that shrouded tall man in a boat
being rowed, alone, closer
and closer to "The Isle of the Dead."

But they are climbing into a white bus,
they'll haunt the shopping mall in a moment.
You still hear the music mourn,
its resonances, a yearning replies
as if to the deep measure of many rivers.
Catch your breath,
which way had you gone?

Live Music in Open Space

Live music heard
      from an open space
still is confining
      and is confined,
irritable drum,
      plucked bass,
ugly the music
      and fearful
gives me the anxiety
      of a child with monsters,
strange faces, the quaint pistol,
      and a wind rising
brings me with a wave
      the music closer—
have me, little wind, turn again
      from these horrors of the day,
lighten my infirmity,
      bring to mind
Julia's dress,
      and Robert Herrick
strolling of old
      in his garden,
her dress that flows
      each way free,
as if she stepped
      to music
down from the immensity.

Whispered in Venus' Ear

See the little ones run away
Some drop and lie there
Some pirouette, then crawl
Some cry out, or do they?
Just watch now, like old gods
From our couches we shall watch
Something finally broke down a century ago
We watch our outcome
From couches we watch
Not unfamiliar with what we watch every year
Indifferent as gods who played with nature
Acquainted as we are
With the crowd being dispersed
With flight across our street
Across our plaza
When a little wind drives
The white globes which are the fallen petals
Of a myrtle tree.

2014

Second Willow Poem

Somewhere along the highway,
My fruits dropped from their sack.
Mankind listens for a bird's night-song,
Soon, huge starlit dogs bark at the Bosphorus.

Still I do not destroy,
Still this is to be a man,
Still with delight the willow rustles,
Not moaning for Ophelia.

Let us lie long deep underground,
Sang the oyster to the whelk.
Let hard-won values be overtaken,
The visits of the drowned girls stop.

To be stone, stone, stone is nothing.
Let them dig us out, we'll show;
My pearl bedding and your spiral
Helped fresh skins run dry for love.

Raw Points

Of anomalies the first, hung on the wall
in the office of a urologist,
an oriole, the berry in its beak
depicted lemon yellow, if for an artist
the Brazilian Pea-Hen sauntered in,
anomaly had fled; elsewhere
on a deathbed Betty was whispering
of wolves invading Antwerp,
so memory now holds fast
Goya's disemboweled horse,
this face that plugs the anus, a fat man's,
then far away, look, my partners drift,
and those I did particularly love—
now to watch them glide, all fireflies,
and father's feet, they cross the organ pedals,
for still I love today, I love today, Echo sang,
and with two fingers branching
father has drawn out the diapason, its flute,
still heard in this sheepfold, diversity
be also praised, vainglory flushed from the wolf-pack.

Gerontion Dreams

Forearm crosses the old-fangled oven lid,
the sleeve of the other
reaching out, taking hold,
shocked by the torment of it all,
by the folly of this love, I vomited
two grey spoonfuls on the black wool.

How dark now. And in this kitchen
what was I to do? On the stair, footsteps,
silence has come,
light footsteps, bringing silence.
Here is a presence, no touch no voice
utter serenity, nothing assured,
nothing asserted.

      …Then with his teeth and hands
tore what he would have written…

Reading Longinus Again

Sappho got it right;
fontanelle and sex do not
interpenetrate. Really
I have seen people, grown intact,
practice a singular
skill, they walk about, they work
in wave patterns of their own.

Bring on the wedding throne;
bring on the island in the sun,
and the sweat is drawn from a body
even by admiration.
Let the sublime come by;
one day I'll see fit
to sense the moving spirit.

This Dark Outside

From down in this dark outside
I hear the old American voices.

Not a candlestick to be seen,
no whiff of roasting hog.

These acts of speech,
while unintelligible,

take on the proper tone
for acts of reverence,

careless that obviously
the good stars hug their orbits.

                    *

Comes the screech of dawn,
a growing progeny

will have begun to shout,
every phrase, almost,

sharp, fast, piercing,
and shrill via the nose,

inflection rising, a harangue
the patois of a threatened self.

For a Minute

Unicorn, leopard in Ash Wednesday,
mole, donkey, lizard and dog,
relish me, relish me fast and soon;
I'll sing of you, carp, to Poulenc's tune,
parked in a pond or the Caspian Sea
beasts of my tiny time, make free
to relish me, feeling in life at home,
bite for a minute, close to the bone.

The Matter of Walls and Ghosts

Walls repugnant or beautiful
sunlit the limestone festooned
with morning glory or honeysuckle
keeping people apart
browned by industrial dirt
gashed by the bullets
old crevices for chickweed and wren
much more when the stories are told
or they are loved for boxing us in
but the ghosts whether fresh or old
cannot commune with them
(no lips to curl in contempt
no tongue to rise and fall)
quiet now the itch to participate
and ghosts that do the talking
they also pronounce the words
that somebody has given them
coupled with virtual breath
in dining-halls, on parapets

White petals molecular still
the posy you saved from the trash
my dear one my companion
scatter them where my ashes went in Bergerac.

Like a Vine in Thy Blood

…tibi rident aequora ponti…
-Lucretius

Since the needle had pricked
its potion into his eyeball
not more than five minutes

the two-door silver car was parked
she stood by the open door
not for the ship under full sail on the skyline

not for the primed canvas
not for the snapshot
for him she smiled and spread her arms

pray do not mistake this poem
drink it in like a margarita
make it happen again in all innocence

pulsing with no end in sight
the kindest gift of chance, freshness
disappears into the momentary and obvious

Nobody's Ezekiel

He felt no spirit penetrate him,
heard no voice persuading him
to get up on his feet and pitilessly speak;
what in heaven then was this—
look up, trees on it that nod to the world
a blue promontory melts into a thunderhead—
brisk as the kingfisher
a warmth was flowing into him,
dense, touching the heart, and radiant—
the Dreamer has let fly with it in a loop,
it sprang away, winged by blood-heat,
it means to target
whomsoever he might single out—
for no time but hers it dwells on her,
distant at the door, not recognizing,
it dwells on her, ageless in her blue, or so
the sick man in the bed
has felt, with an affect so wild
that where she steps ashore, all foam, no feeling,
the crystal shrine is taking shape, he longs for her.

Amor-Shakti
nursed it, Memory weans it,
now circling this other and his person
it hovers, it is appealing, near
with a perfection
not beyond reckoning.

Fragment

Even if I'd known what you wanted to hear from me
I'd have disappointed you.
                Only in the night,
toward a certain pitch
of loneliness,
               believe me, the dark sweltered
a marvel for you.
            A mockingbird was
inventing a song, it sang on and on;
not a note in imitation,
the song conjugated trills delicate and furious,
melodies broken beyond repair;
it sang to bring the thunder on
                and it sang the more
the louder the storm, thicker fell
sheets and sheets of rain.

That was a night in the back of beyond.
Silence becomes you.

There he is, again
         the little owl,
                 calling to you.

Caducity

The Kirghiz Steppes
    in old photos
        crumpled brown paper

Garden of Hotel Asia Minor
    sparse lawn, at the center
        the dry fountain

Steppes once with an earth spell
    (regardless of wars)
        could bind the traveller

Garden where in memory
    the tenant's lame wife
        serves breakfast with heart

All over crumpled brown paper
    the traveller was laying
        roll on roll of film

On sparse lawn a few friends
    and strangers we took pleasure
        in every next thing.

Age stuns heaping regrets
    sparky crock still a puzzle
        missing pieces.

It never hurts to love again
    of all pieces when
        did spirit steal that one

Eurydice Perceived

...the singing insect whose records
are inscribed in our coal-seams.
J.-H. Fabre

What if I never again for once could see
her strict small face brighten to a gift
What if I tipped the attic windows open
and never woke again to birdsong rushing up
Torched by curiosity even as I caught my breath
I let the forelock of a moment slip
so rare a time that idled is

A moment captured strikes you unawares
but grows a form gradually in afterthought

Wait: in immediacy akin to music
unlike music the moments change their form
And even music loved but heard distractedly
a ton of times weighs never quite the same

So in a shroud the figure lifted
                    now most herself
shocked by the light out there incipient
her gaunt features were shaping to smile

What end then spells out the stuffs in variance?
What were the words that came to grandfather?
It is the quality of the affection
that carves in a mind the trace...

I trace values on a map until the end
Let the quality, gods, of affection
go deep as the clarity of grandfather's eyes
When memory in a moment shifts its parallel
I'll see and hear again re-opening the question

Even if Eros with a tusk scatters her garden
O predecessors you who teach restraint
with the grasshopper's voice our whispers blend
yours console in the shadow of her pergolas

Baudelaire's 'Le Flacon' Unrhymed

Perfumes exist that find all matter porous,
it might be said they penetrate even glass.
Open a coffer come from the Orient—
The lock scrapes, the key yelps and sticks,

But just as in an abandoned house, secreted
in an armoire an antiquated bottle,
a souvenir, retained a heavy scent,
there's life in it, out spurts a living soul.

A swarm of thoughts, twilight chrysalids,
gently shudders, spreads wings, takes flight,
tinctures of blue, frozen rose, blades of gold,
and memory is there, intoxicating.

It twists, it turns in the commotions
of air, with both hands thrusting a dizzied
and defeated soul to the very lip
of an abyss the human atmospheres obscure,

and spills it where for an age the abyss has been
for reeking Lazarus to tear the shroud away
making to move his spectre of a corpse,
spellbinding, the sepulchral love long gone.

Just so, lost to all human memory
I'll be tossed aside, decrepit,
a squalid, sticky, cracked old bottle;
yet I'll be witness to your force,

amiable pestilence, and of your viciousness,
liquor that angels concocted, cherished venom
eating at me, my life and death of heart—
still for you I'll be a winding-sheet.

The Springtime Garden Fair

What coombs of flowers
and canvas booths, the giant
snowdrop, imponderable orchid,
these hats and daffodils, azure of spiderwort,
all appeal, but for what
while the Virgin on a tin plate tilts her head,
and the young women—
don't go too close,
how love again is multiplied
and flesh clings,
freedom is not in these legs
a little tanned already,
and you are too old
to leap from this vehicle,
gone on shapeliness, gone all over again.

Smoke Over the Rose Garden

Here's a seamstress holds her ground,
incipient pyramids to be seen far off,
and to be stitched, still further off,
with sinew the cured antelope skin.

On the couturier now she turns her back,
worldlywise cross-legged she squats:
then she floats her square of cotton,
smoothes it, makes a fold, and pins,
pins more and stitches, floats again
soon to be stitched the cotton square.

Arctic against Norway an ocean crashes,
the shooter aims his automatic, and this year
death has already undone so many.

Still the seamstress busies herself,
absorbed in stitching, a pleasure to watch;
choosing at random this animal or that,
some few climb up to ride in the carousel,
round and round, the carousel of cultures.

I went in search of the strange,
of the original sometimes. Dawn
would come there with a different light.
There would be time to admire the marvels.

A rose garden is planted,
a rose garden, with roses
of different shades, different fragrances,
the older the sweeter, white or red
(O France, O fragrance) the more petals
the more inscrutable, faint in the memory.

A rose garden is planted
to be loitered in for a moment,
or sauntered through
in measure to the freedom of an afternoon.

Sparing no time to fathom later the substance
in reminiscence, deaf or too distracted to hear
the hidden laughter,
I must have raced through many gardens;
I heave and heave, only for glowing cinders.

Chopin

So much about him said and done,
so much from his numbers, textures
drawn by the tips of such fingers
as those of Cortot, Lipatti, Rubinstein
still to have remained for us
immaculate, note by note,

phrase by phrase, particles flow,
none goes to waste in their metamorphosis:
beads of sweat dot Sappho's upper lip,
and the bride gone so soon, we quell the sublime.

Come from the powers that aim
danger and love at us,
what can the Muse
have been thinking of,
so to live among us, giving,
giving and giving.

Lost Squadron

Often enough
strapped, sedentary
in the cockpit of my biplane,
I dropped sputtering to earth.

To rise from the waters
Icarus made no effort;
flight like his, for a second or two
seeing the islands, warships,
mountains and city, people crawling. . .
but life primes itself with legend.

It stared me in the face,
my furrow did. In my wallet,
olives, bread, cheese, and water
cool in the shade,
safely aged.

Allow my distance, daughter,
when I see, from the riverside,
a tribe of cormorants
fly in their formation
as some few friends once did
in their lost squadron.

Notes

"Rain Crow": Rain Crow is the byname, current in rustic Central Texas, for the yellow-billed cuckoo.

"Live Music in Open Space": "Each way free" is quoted from Robert Herrick, "On Julia's Clothes."

"Gerontion Dreams": The closing lines vary lines 11-12 of Byron's "A Dream" (Pt.3).

"Nobody's Ezekiel": "blue promontory" comes from *Anthony and Cleopatra* (IV,4). "Shakti" in the Sanskrit Vedanta is a potency originating in Brahma; a person mediating it brings healing and fertility, but then it benefits the "Great Illusion" (Maya).

"Baudelaire, 'Le Flacon'": Translated without reference to or memory of existing translations.

Other Books by Christopher Middleton
Published by Sheep Meadow Press

Forty Days in The Calypso Saloon & Frescos with Graffiti (2013)

Just Look at the Dancers: Canticles, Fumes, Monostichs (2012)

A Company of Ghosts (2011)

The Tenor on Horseback: Poems (2007)

Tankard Cat (2005)

Of the Mortal Fire: Poems 1999-2002 (2003)

The Word Pavilion and Selected Poems (2001)

Prose by Christopher Middleton

Pataxanadu and Other Prose (Carcanet 1977)

Serpentine (Oasis Books 1985)

In the Mirror of the Eighth King (Green Integer 1999)

Crypto-topographia: Stories of Secret Places (Enitharmon Press 2002)

Depictions of Blaff (Green Integer 2010)

Loose Cannons (University of New Mexico Press 2014)